★ ★

Veterans Day

Arlene Worsley

Weigl Publishers Inc.

Published by Weigl Publishers Inc.
350 5th Avenue, 59th Floor
New York, NY 10118
Website: www.weigl.com

Library of Congress Cataloging-in-Publication Data

Worsley, Arlene.
  Veterans Day / Arlene Worsley.
      p. cm. -- (American holidays)
  Includes index.
  ISBN 978-1-59036-406-2 (hard cover : alk. paper) -- ISBN 978-1-59036-409-3 (soft cover : alk. paper)
  1. Veterans Day. 2. Holidays--United States. I. Title. II. American holidays (New York, N.Y.)
  D671.W67 2006
  394.264--dc22
                                     2005029037

Printed in the United States in North Mankato, Minnesota
2 3 4 5 6 7 8 9 0 13 12 11 10 09

122009
WEP 17000

Editor Heather C. Hudak
Design and Layout Terry Paulhus

Cover On Veterans Day, parade
participants include military units,
marching bands, veterans groups,
military vehicles, and flag teams.

Contents

Introduction

★ ★

On this day, Americans honor war veterans who served in all wars.

DID YOU KNOW?

Today, there are more than 25 million war veterans living in the United States.

November 11 is Veterans Day. In 1918, it was the day a peace agreement was signed to end World War I.

Veterans Day is observed every year in the United States. On this day, Americans honor war **veterans** who served in all wars. Americans also honor those who served on military missions to maintain peace in warring countries.

On Veterans Day, special events take place at war **memorials** across the United States. Veterans, soldiers, and citizens place flowers and flags on graves. Some people quietly pay their respects at private services. Veterans Day is a time to give thanks to all those who have served to protect America's freedom.

At the Vietnam Veterans Memorial Wall, there are 58,249 names of those who died and those who remain missing from the Vietnam War. The wall is located in Washington, DC.

World War I

★ ★

Millions of Americans served in World War I.

DID YOU KNOW?

More than 20,000 women took part in World War I. They belonged to the Army and Navy Nurse Corps, the Marine Corps, and the Coast Guard.

A war broke out in Europe in 1914. This war involved almost every country in the world. It was called the Great War. Today, the Great War is known as World War I.

The United States joined the war in 1917. Millions of Americans served in the war. Armed forces fought in trenches. These were forts dug deep into the ground. Trenches were one of the most dangerous points of combat.

World War I marked the first use of chemical weapons. These are weapons containing harmful substances, such as poison. It was also the first time airplanes attacked people from the sky. More than 116,000 American soldiers lost their lives in the Great War.

Life in the trenches was harsh. Trenches were often drenched in water and crawling with rats, frogs, and lice. Soldiers were constantly exposed to harmful diseases.

Fourteen Points

★ ★

President Woodrow Wilson outlined his goals to end the war.

DID YOU KNOW?

President Wilson's quest for peace led to the creation of the League of Nations in 1919. This was an organization that promoted international cooperation. In 1946, the United Nations replaced the League

On January 8, 1918, President Woodrow Wilson gave an important speech to **Congress**. He outlined his goals to end the war. These became known as the Fourteen Points.

President Wilson wanted cooperation from all countries involved. To achieve peace between nations, he encouraged freedom to cross the seas and to return **independence** to occupied lands. President Wilson also wanted to limit the use of weapons and maintain the right of independent countries to govern their own people.

President Wilson's Fourteen Points became the basis of Germany's **surrender** in November 1918. They also formed the foundation of the League of Nations, the world's first international peace organization.

A Just and Lasting Peace

President Woodrow Wilson believed that if all the world's nations worked together, they could achieve world peace.

"It is that the world be made fit and safe to live in; and particularly that it be made safe for every peace-loving nation which, like our own, wishes to live its own life, determine its own institutions, be assured of justice and fair dealing by the other peoples of the world as against force and selfish aggression. All the peoples of the world are in effect partners in this interest, and for our own part we see very clearly that unless justice be done to others, it will not be done to us. The program of the world's peace, therefore, is our program."

—President Woodrow Wilson

President Woodrow Wilson was awarded the Nobel Prize for Peace in 1919.

War is Over

★ ★

World War I came to a close on November 11, 1918.

After four years, World War I came to a close on November 11, 1918. The Armistice Treaty was signed to end the war. This was a peace agreement between Germany and the **Allied Powers**.

In the United States, many people lined the streets celebrating the victory. Americans danced and cheered as bells and whistles sounded. Businesses also closed for the day.

Americans wanted to remember those who died in the war. Memorials were built in cities, towns, and villages. In 1919, President Woodrow Wilson named November 11 Armistice Day.

★ ★ ★ ★ ★ ★ ★ ★ ★ ★
The telegram sent to the front line of battle ordered troops to stop fighting at 5:00 A.M. on November 11, 1918.

The Armistice Treaty was signed at 5:00 AM on a railroad carriage in Rethondes, France. The war ended six hours later.

One hour after the announcement of the war's end, there were street celebrations in

Creating the Holiday

★ ★

Armistice Day became a national holiday in 1938.

From 1919 to 1954, November 11 was called Armistice Day. The United States Congress made Armistice Day a national holiday in 1938.

Raymond Weeks, an American **patriot**, organized the first Armistice Day parade in 1947. It was held in Birmingham, Alabama. He wanted to honor "all of America's veterans for their loyal service." President Dwight D. Eisenhower changed the name of the holiday to Veterans Day in 1954. Now, every year on the 11th hour, of the 11th day, of the 11th month, Americans remember their heroes of war and of peace.

★ ★ ★ ★ ★ ★ ★ ★ ★
Dwight D. Eisenhower served as a supreme commander in World War II.

War medals are symbols of patriotism, courage, and sacrifice.

Veterans Day is a day to remember war heroes from all wars. It is also a day to honor the brave military personnel who defend the United States today.

Veterans Day Today

★ ★

Cities and towns all over the country have parades and ceremonies.

On Veterans Day, cities and towns all over the country have parades and ceremonies. An important national ceremony is at the Tomb of the Unknowns in Arlington, Virginia.

During the ceremony, the president of the United States lays a wreath on the tomb. He then steps back and salutes. A bugler plays *Taps*. This song is a farewell to those who died in war.

National Veterans Awareness Week is held one week before Veterans Day. Students learn about how veterans helped defend America's freedom.

★ ★ ★ ★ ★ ★ ★ ★ ★

After the bugler plays *Taps*, many veterans groups march in the Parade of Flags inside the Memorial Amphitheater.

The Tomb of the Unknowns is located in Arlington National Cemetery. It has been the United States' military cemetery since 1864. More than 300,000 people are buried there. Public ceremonies are held at the Memorial Amphitheater. The cemetery also has many **monuments** and memorials. These include the Nurses Memorial, the President John F. Kennedy Gravesite, and the Space Shuttle "Challenger" Memorial.

Arlington National Cemetery is a resting place for veterans from all the nation's wars.

Americans Remember

Veterans Day is celebrated all over the United States. Many Americans visit war memorials and cemeteries. Veterans are also invited to local schools to talk about their war experience.

San Francisco, California

The annual Veterans Day ceremony in Honolulu, Hawai'i, is at the National Memorial Cemetery of the Pacific. Many people also visit the USS *Arizona* Memorial in Pearl Harbor. They remember the soldiers who defended America's freedom during World War II.

In San Francisco, California, there was a week-long Veterans Day celebration in 2000. Many people visited the *Moving Wall*. This is a traveling wall that contains engraved names of American soldiers who lost their lives in the Vietnam War. It is half the size of the war memorial in Washington, DC.

0   100   200   300 miles

Honolulu, Hawai'i

Each year in Branson, Missouri, there is a week-long celebration called the Veterans Homecoming. It is known as "America's largest Veterans Day celebration." Activities range from hot air balloon rides to formal ceremonies.

Arlington, Virginia

Branson, Missouri

Every year on Veterans Day, thousands of Americans visit the Tomb of the Unknowns in Arlington, Virginia. Since 1937, the 3rd United States Infantry guards the tomb 24 hours a day and seven days a week. Serving as a sentinel, or tomb guard, is considered one of the highest honors for soldiers.

Holiday Symbols

Special symbols of remembrance can be found in many parts of the United States. These symbols are meant to honor the country's wartime dead and living. They also help to remind Americans of the great **sacrifices** people made for their country's freedom.

Memorials

One of the most important memorials is the United States Marine Corps Memorial. It is located in Washington, DC. The statue shows the raising of the United States flag atop Mount Suribachi in Japan during World War II. It is dedicated to the U.S. Marine Corps, who have defended the United States since 1775.

★ ★ ★ ★ ★ ★ ★ ★ ★

At the request of President John F. Kennedy in 1961, a cloth United States flag flies atop the 60-foot bronze flagpole.

Tomb of the Unknowns

The tomb contains the remains of unknown American soldiers who died in World War I, World War II, the Korean War, and the Vietnam War. These soldiers stand for every American who has died for their country. The tomb serves as America's promise to peace and freedom. More than 4 million Americans visit the tomb each year.

Poppies

After World War I, an American named Moina Michael began selling paper poppies. The money she raised was used to support war veterans. The poppy became an official memorial flower in 1922. Americans wear poppies on their coats and hats to honor those who served the United States in war and in peace.

Further Research

There are many books and websites about Veterans Day. These resources will help you learn more about the history and traditions of Veterans Day.

Websites

To learn more about the history and traditions of Veterans Day, visit:

www1.va.gov/opa/vetsday

To learn more about Arlington National Cemetery, visit:

www.arlingtoncemetery.org

Books

Brill, Marlene Targ and Qi Z. Wang. *Veterans Day*. Minnesota: First Avenue Editions, 2002.

Hatt, Christine. *World War I, 1914-18*. London: Franklin Watts, 2001.

Crafts and Recipes

Thank You Card

Thank you cards are a great way to let local war veterans know how much you appreciate them. To begin, fold a piece of construction paper in half to make a card. On the front of the card, draw a picture that shows your feelings about Veterans Day. On the inside of the card, write a thank you message or a poem about war and peace. Send the card to your local branch of the American Legion.

Memorial Poppy Arrangement

Before going to a Veterans Day ceremony, make a small poppy arrangement. To begin, you will need a small, woven basket. Bunch one newspaper page into a ball, and place it at the bottom of the basket. Flatten the newspaper ball. Then, place a round piece of styrofoam into the basket. With an adult, use pins to attach handmade red poppies all over the styrofoam. Make sure there are no visible spaces. To finish, insert a small U.S. flag to the side of the styrofoam. At the ceremony, you can give the poppy arrangement to a war veteran or place it on a gravestone of your choice.

Veterans Day Recipe

Berry Shortcake

Ingredients:

6 cups of berries

8 ready-made English biscuits

1 cup of ready-made whipped cream

4 tablespoons of sugar

Equipment:

large bowl

whisk

8 saucer plates

1. Wash the berries. Place the berries in a large bowl.
2. Sprinkle sugar over the berries. Gently stir the berries and sugar together with a tablespoon.
3. On each individual saucer plate, add two tablespoons of berries. Scoop one heaping tablespoon of whipped cream on the center of the berries.
4. Place one ready-made biscuit on top of the whipped cream on each plate.
5. Add one tablespoon of berries to the top of the biscuits. Then, scoop one tablespoon of whipped cream on top of the berries.
6. Top with one berry. Serve these berry shortcakes to family and friends.

Veterans Day Quiz

What have you learned about Veterans Day? See if you can answer the following questions. Check your answers on the next page.

2 At what time on Veterans Day do Americans have a moment of silence?

1 Where is the Tomb of the Unknowns?

4 Which war is known as the Great War?

3 On which instrument is *Taps* usually played?

5 What was Veterans Day first called?

On Veterans Day, thousands of veterans and their families visit the Vietnam Veterans Memorial.

Fascinating Facts

★ The first poppy factory in the United States was built in 1924. It opened in Pittsburgh, Pennsylvania. The factory was built to make poppies for Memorial Day and Veterans Day. Veterans help put together poppies. Today, this poppy factory distributes about 14 million poppies around the world.

★ The Tomb of the Unknowns holds the graves of four unknown soldiers. The first unknown soldier was buried in 1921.

★ In the United States, about 1.7 million veterans are women.

★ The National World War II Memorial was opened on April 29, 2004. It is located in Washington, DC. The memorial honors the Americans who served and died in World War II. It also honors those who supported the war effort at home.

Quiz Answers:
1. The Tomb of the Unknowns is at Arlington, Virginia.
2. Americans have a moment of silence at 11:00 AM on Veterans Day.
3. *Taps* is played on a bugle.
4. The Great War is also known as World War I.
5. Veterans Day was first called Armistice Day.

Glossary

★ ★ ★ ★ ★ ★ ★ ★ ★ ★ ★ ★ ★ ★ ★ ★

Allied Powers: a military partnership during World War I of 28 countries in opposition to another group of countries

Congress: a governing body of the United States

independence: freedom from control

memorials: places where people who have died are laid to rest

monuments: large stones or statues built as lasting public tributes to a person, a group of people, or event

patriot: a person who loves and supports the country they live in

sacrifices: valuable things given up for a special cause

surrender: to declare defeat

tradition: a custom or way of doing something every year

veterans: people who have served in war

Index

★ ★ ★ ★ ★ ★ ★ ★ ★ ★ ★ ★ ★ ★ ★ ★